The Very Best of Friedrich Nietzsche

Quotes from a Great Thinker

DAVID GRAHAM

Copyright © 2014 David Graham

All rights reserved.

ISBN: 1502466325
ISBN-13: 978-1502466327

DISCLAIMER

Although every effort has been taken to ensure all information in this book is accurate, human error is always a possibility and therefore the author apologises in the event of any inaccuracies.

CONTENTS

Introduction	1
About God & Religion	3
About Himself	9
About Mankind	11
About Women	19
Art & Music	23
Friends & Enemies	27
General Philosophy	29
Life & Death	51
Love, Marriage & Relationships	55

INTRODUCTION

One of the greatest minds of his time, Friedrich Nietzsche is probably one of the best known names in philosophy. Ahead of his times in many ways, he was also arguably the most outspoken atheist of the 19th century; indeed, many of his quotes suggest he was not just without religion, but against it.

Nietzsche was, and still is, greatly revered much due to the boldness of his words, his ability to articulate life and existence in a very unique way and his literary works. Among other subjects, he wrote many texts on morality, religion, philosophy and science.

In 1889, aged just 44, Nietzsche suffered severe brain damage following a collapse. Though he lived until 1900, he never regained his mental faculties following this collapse. Though at the time the cause was believed to be tertiary syphilis, it is now known with almost certainty that his breakdown and ultimate death was actually due to brain cancer.

Following his death, Nietzsche's works became associated with negative connotations, such as Nazi ideology. This was in fact due to his sister's reworking of his unpublished writings, in order to encompass her own ideology, much of which ran in complete contrast to Nietzsche's opinions; he was known to explicitly oppose anti-semitism and nationalism.

Thanks to the recent realisation of the falsity of his sister's reworkings, Nietzsche is as much admired today as he was during his own time. He is a very much quoted figure; there are few alive today who have never heard some variation of his saying, 'that which does not kill us makes us stronger'.

This book brings together some of Nietzsche's most notable and interesting quotes on a variety of subjects.

ABOUT GOD & RELIGION

"Is man one of God's blunders? Or is God one of man's blunders?"

*

"The 'kingdom of Heaven' is a condition of the heart - not something that comes 'upon the earth' or 'after death.'"

*

"There cannot be a God because if there were one, I could not believe that I was not He."

DAVID GRAHAM

*

"I cannot believe in a God who wants to be praised all the time."

*

"There is in general good reason to suppose that in several respects the gods could all benefit from instruction by us human beings. We humans are - more humane."

*

"There is not enough love and goodness in the world to permit giving any of it away to imaginary beings."

*

"The Christian resolution to find the world ugly and bad has made the world ugly and bad."

*

"Whoever feels predestined to see and not to believe

will find all believers too noisy and pushy: he guards against them."

*

"After coming into contact with a religious man I always feel I must wash my hands."

*

"God is a thought who makes crooked all that is straight."

*

"There are people who want to make men's lives more difficult for no other reason than the chance it provides them afterwards to offer their prescription for alleviating life; their Christianity, for instance."

*

"In heaven, all the interesting people are missing."

*

"Faith: not wanting to know what is true."

*

"I would believe only in a God that knows how to Dance."

*

"Every church is a stone on the grave of a god-man: it does not want him to rise up again under any circumstances."

*

"A subject for a great poet would be God's boredom after the seventh day of creation."

*

"A casual stroll through the lunatic asylum shows that faith does not prove anything."

*

"Today I love myself as I love my god: who could charge me with a sin today? I know only sins against my god; but who knows my god?"

*

"In Christianity neither morality nor religion come into contact with reality at any point."

*

"The word 'Christianity' is already a misunderstanding - in reality there has been only one Christian, and he died on the Cross."

*

"There is not enough religion in the world even to destroy religion."

*

DAVID GRAHAM

"Once spirit was God, then it became man, and now
it is even becoming mob."

ABOUT HIMSELF

"The aphorism in which I am the first master among Germans, are the forms of 'eternity'; my ambition is to say in ten sentences what everyone else says in a book - what everyone else does not say in a book."

*

"I love those who do not know how to live for today."

*

"Of all that is written, I love only what a person has written with his own blood."

DAVID GRAHAM

*

"Whenever I climb I am followed by a dog called 'Ego'."

ABOUT MANKIND

"The doer alone learneth."

*

"The most common lie is that which one lies to himself; lying to others is relatively an exception."

*

"In the consciousness of the truth he has perceived, man now sees everywhere only the awfulness or the absurdity of existence and loathing seizes him."

*

"There is nothing we like to communicate to others as much as the seal of secrecy together with what lies under it."

*

"Anyone who has declared someone else to be an idiot, a bad apple, is annoyed when it turns out in the end that he isn't."

*

"Many a man fails as an original thinker simply because his memory it too good."

*

"What can everyone do? Praise and blame. This is human virtue, this is human madness."

*

"People who have given us their complete confidence believe that they have a right to ours. The inference is false, a gift confers no rights."

*

"What then in the last resort are the truths of mankind? They are the irrefutable errors of mankind."

*

"No one lies so boldly as the man who is indignant."

*

"The individual has always had to struggle to keep from being overwhelmed by the tribe. If you try it, you will be lonely often, and sometimes frightened. But no price is too high to pay for the privilege of owning yourself."

*

"Nothing is beautiful, only man: on this piece of naivete rests all aesthetics, it is the first truth of aesthetics. Let us immediately add its second: nothing is ugly but degenerate man - the domain of aesthetic judgment is therewith defined."

*

"He who cannot give anything away cannot feel anything either."

*

"Whoever has provoked men to rage against him has always gained a party in his favor, too."

*

"'Evil men have no songs.' How is it that the Russians have songs?"

*

"Not necessity, not desire - no, the love of power is the demon of men. Let them have everything - health, food, a place to live, entertainment - they are and remain unhappy and low-spirited: for the demon waits and waits and will be satisfied."

*

"Every man is a creative cause of what happens, a primum mobile with an original movement."

*

"When one has not had a good father, one must create one."

*

"The true man wants two things: danger and play. For that reason he wants woman, as the most dangerous plaything."

*

"The surest way to corrupt a youth is to instruct him to hold in higher esteem those who think alike than those who think differently."

*

"The abdomen is the reason why man does not readily take himself to be a god."

*

"In the last analysis, even the best man is evil: in the last analysis, even the best woman is bad."

*

"Fanatics are picturesque, mankind would rather see gestures than listen to reasons."

*

"Perhaps I know best why it is man alone who laughs; he alone suffers so deeply that he had to invent laughter."

*

"What is good? All that heightens the feeling of power, the will to power, power itself in man."

*

"Many are stubborn in pursuit of the path they have chosen, few in pursuit of the goal."

*

"When a hundred men stand together, each of them loses his mind and gets another one."

*

"Whoever has witnessed another's ideal becomes his inexorable judge and as it were his evil conscience."

*

"There are horrible people who, instead of solving a problem, tangle it up and make it harder to solve for anyone who wants to deal with it. Whoever does not know how to hit the nail on the head should be asked not to hit it at all."

*

"In the course of history, men come to see that iron necessity is neither iron nor necessary."

DAVID GRAHAM

*

"There are slavish souls who carry their appreciation for favors done them so far that they strangle themselves with the rope of gratitude."

*

"Whoever despises himself nonetheless respects himself as one who despises."

*

"Our treasure lies in the beehive of our knowledge. We are perpetually on the way thither, being by nature winged insects and honey gatherers of the mind."

*

"In every real man a child is hidden that wants to play."

ABOUT WOMEN

"If a woman possesses manly virtues one should run away from her; and if she does not possess them she runs away from herself."

*

"Behind all their personal vanity, women themselves always have an impersonal contempt for woman."

*

"Woman was God's second mistake."

*

"Stupid as a man, say the women: cowardly as a woman, say the men. Stupidity in a woman is unwomanly."

*

"Women are considered deep - why? Because one can never discover any bottom to them. Women are not even shallow."

*

"It is the most sensual men who need to flee women and torment their bodies."

*

"For the woman, the man is a means: the end is always the child."

*

"Ah, women. They make the highs higher and the lows more frequent."

"Genteel women suppose that those things do not really exist about which it is impossible to talk in polite company."

ART & MUSIC

"An artist has no home in Europe except in Paris."

*

"Art raises its head where creeds relax."

*

"We have art in order not to die of the truth."

*

"The essence of all beautiful art, all great art, is

gratitude."

*

"When art dresses in worn-out material it is most easily recognized as art."

*

"Art is the proper task of life."

*

"Admiration for a quality or an art can be so strong that it deters us from striving to possess it."

*

"Art is not merely an imitation of the reality of nature, but in truth a metaphysical supplement to the reality of nature, placed alongside thereof for its conquest."

*

"For art to exist, for any sort of aesthetic activity to exist, a certain physiological precondition is indispensable: intoxication."

*

"The bad gains respect through imitation, the good loses it especially in art."

*

"In music the passions enjoy themselves."

FRIENDS & ENEMIES

"Shared joys make a friend, not shared sufferings."

*

"A good writer possesses not only his own spirit but also the spirit of his friends."

*

"The best weapon against an enemy is another enemy."

*

"The man of knowledge must be able not only to love his enemies but also to hate his friends."

*

"A friend should be a master at guessing and keeping still: you must not want to see everything."

*

"Rejoicing in our joy, not suffering over our suffering, makes someone a friend."

*

"Go up close to your friend, but do not go over to him! We should also respect the enemy in our friend."

GENERAL PHILOSOPHY

"We do not hate as long as we still attach a lesser value, but only when we attach an equal or a greater value."

*

"What really raises one's indignation against suffering is not suffering intrinsically, but the senselessness of suffering."

*

"What? You seek something? You wish to multiply yourself tenfold, a hundredfold? You seek followers? Seek zeros!"

*

"There is more wisdom in your body than in your deepest philosophy."

*

"Hope in reality is the worst of all evils because it prolongs the torments of man."

*

"To use the same words is not a sufficient guarantee of understanding; one must use the same words for the same genus of inward experience; ultimately one must have one's experiences in common."

*

"You have your way. I have my way. As for the right way, the correct way, and the only way, it does not exist."

*

"Convictions are more dangerous foes of truth than lies."

*

"Whoever does not have a good father should procure one."

*

"Existence really is an imperfect tense that never becomes a present."

*

"Before the effect one believes in different causes than one does after the effect."

*

"What do you regard as most humane? To spare someone shame."

*

"The desire to annoy no one, to harm no one, can equally well be the sign of a just as of an anxious disposition."

*

"The best author will be the one who is ashamed to become a writer."

*

"We should consider every day lost on which we have not danced at least once. And we should call every truth false which was not accompanied by at least one laugh."

*

"When one has a great deal to put into it a day has a hundred pockets."

*

"There is a rollicking kindness that looks like malice."

*

"War has always been the grand sagacity of every spirit which has grown too inward and too profound; its curative power lies even in the wounds one receives."

*

"I do not know what the spirit of a philosopher could more wish to be than a good dancer. For the dance is his ideal, also his fine art, finally also the only kind of piety he knows, his 'divine service.'"

*

"There are no moral phenomena at all, but only a moral interpretation of phenomena."

*

"I assess the power of a will by how much resistance, pain, torture it endures and knows how to turn to its advantage."

*

"When one does away with oneself one does the most estimable thing possible: one thereby almost deserves to live."

*

"Undeserved praise causes more pangs of conscience later than undeserved blame, but probably only for this reason, that our power of judgment are more completely exposed by being over praised than by being unjustly underestimated."

*

"It is not when truth is dirty, but when it is shallow, that the lover of knowledge is reluctant to step into its waters."

*

"Our vanity is hardest to wound precisely when our pride has just been wounded."

*

"On the mountains of truth you can never climb in vain: either you will reach a point higher up today, or you will be training your powers so that you will be able to climb higher tomorrow."

*

"When you look into an abyss, the abyss also looks into you."

*

"Words are but symbols for the relations of things to one another and to us; nowhere do they touch upon absolute truth."

*

"Judgments, value judgments concerning life, for or against, can in the last resort never be true: they possess value only as symptoms, they come into consideration only as symptoms - in themselves such judgments are stupidities."

*

"Great indebtedness does not make men grateful, but vengeful; and if a little charity is not forgotten, it turns into a gnawing worm."

*

"You say it is the good cause that hallows even war? I say unto you: it is the good war that hallows any cause."

*

"At times one remains faithful to a cause only because its opponents do not cease to be insipid."

*

"Necessity is not an established fact, but an interpretation."

*

"Morality is the herd-instinct in the individual."

*

"It is good to express a thing twice right at the outset and so to give it a right foot and also a left one. Truth can surely stand on one leg, but with two it will be able to walk and get around."

*

"In large states public education will always be mediocre, for the same reason that in large kitchens the cooking is usually bad."

*

"One often contradicts an opinion when what is uncongenial is really the tone in which it was conveyed."

*

"Success has always been a great liar."

*

"When one has finished building one's house, one suddenly realizes that in the process one has learned something that one really needed to know in the worst way - before one began."

*

"He who has a why to live can bear almost any how."

*

"The future influences the present just as much as the past."

*

"It says nothing against the ripeness of a spirit that it has a few worms."

*

"In individuals, insanity is rare; but in groups, parties, nations and epochs, it is the rule."

*

"There are no eternal facts, as there are no absolute truths."

*

"One has to pay dearly for immortality; one has to die several times while one is still alive."

*

"All things are subject to interpretation; whichever interpretation prevails at a given time is a function of power and not truth."

*

"The press, the machine, the railway, the telegraph are premises whose thousand-year conclusion no one has yet dared to draw."

*

"Idleness is the parent of psychology."

*

"Mystical explanations are thought to be deep; the truth is that they are not even shallow."

*

"Some are made modest by great praise, others insolent."

*

"All truth is simple... is that not doubly a lie?"

*

"There are no facts, only interpretations."

*

"Wit is the epitaph of an emotion."

*

"Fear is the mother of morality."

*

"Talking much about oneself can also be a means to conceal oneself."

*

"Nothing has been purchased more dearly than the little bit of reason and sense of freedom which now constitutes our pride."

*

"If there is something to pardon in everything, there is also something to condemn."

*

"Although the most acute judges of the witches and

even the witches themselves, were convinced of the guilt of witchery, the guilt nevertheless was non-existent. It is thus with all guilt."

*

"Those who cannot understand how to put their thoughts on ice should not enter into the heat of debate."

*

"To be ashamed of one's immorality: that is a step on the staircase at whose end one is also ashamed of one's morality."

*

"In everything one thing is impossible: rationality."

*

"One ought to hold on to one's heart; for if one lets it go, one soon loses control of the head too."

"It is impossible to suffer without making someone pay for it; every complaint already contains revenge."

*

"Extreme positions are not succeeded by moderate ones, but by contrary extreme positions."

*

"Does wisdom perhaps appear on the earth as a raven which is inspired by the smell of carrion?"

*

"We hear only those questions for which we are in a position to find answers."

*

"All credibility, all good conscience, all evidence of truth come only from the senses."

*

"Whoever fights monsters should see to it that in the process he does not become a monster. And if you gaze long enough into an abyss, the abyss will gaze back into you."

*

"He who would learn to fly one day must first learn to stand and walk and run and climb and dance; one cannot fly into flying."

*

"Sleeping is no mean art: for its sake one must stay awake all day."

*

"Do whatever you will, but first be such as are able to will."

*

"To forget one's purpose is the commonest form of stupidity."

*

"That which does not kill us makes us stronger."

*

"He that humbleth himself wishes to be exalted."

*

"Glance into the world just as though time were gone: and everything crooked will become straight to you."

*

"Experience, as a desire for experience, does not come off. We must not study ourselves while having an experience."

*

"Blessed are the forgetful: for they get the better even of their blunders."

*

"There are various eyes. Even the Sphinx has eyes: and as a result there are various truths, and as a result there is no truth."

*

"One may sometimes tell a lie, but the grimace that accompanies it tells the truth."

*

"A great value of antiquity lies in the fact that its writings are the only ones that modern men still read with exactness."

*

"Egoism is the very essence of a noble soul."

"All truly great thoughts are conceived by walking."

*

"We often refuse to accept an idea merely because the tone of voice in which it has been expressed is unsympathetic to us."

*

"All sciences are now under the obligation to prepare the ground for the future task of the philosopher, which is to solve the problem of value, to determine the true hierarchy of values."

*

"He who laughs best today, will also laugh last."

*

"In praise there is more obtrusiveness than in blame."

*

"Plato was a bore."

*

"Arrogance on the part of the meritorious is even more offensive to us than the arrogance of those without merit: for merit itself is offensive."

*

"The irrationality of a thing is no argument against its existence, rather a condition of it."

*

"The world itself is the will to power - and nothing else! And you yourself are the will to power - and nothing else!"

*

"The lie is a condition of life."

*

"Character is determined more by the lack of certain experiences than by those one has had."

*

"There is an innocence in admiration; it is found in those to whom it has never yet occurred that they, too, might be admired some day."

*

"One must still have chaos in oneself to be able to give birth to a dancing star."

*

"Thoughts are the shadows of our feelings - always darker, emptier and simpler."

LIFE & DEATH

"Let us beware of saying that death is the opposite of life. The living being is only a species of the dead, and a very rare species."

*

"We love life, not because we are used to living but because we are used to loving."

*

"He who fights with monsters might take care lest he thereby become a monster. Is not life a hundred times too short for us to bore ourselves?"

*

"One should die proudly when it is no longer possible to live proudly."

*

"Regarding life, the wisest men of all ages have judged alike: it is worthless."

*

"To live is to suffer, to survive is to find some meaning in the suffering."

*

"Without music, life would be a mistake."

*

"Is life not a thousand times too short for us to bore ourselves?"

*

"I still live, I still think: I still have to live, for I still have to think."

*

"It is always consoling to think of suicide: in that way one gets through many a bad night."

LOVE, MARRIAGE & RELATIONSHIPS

"This is what is hardest: to close the open hand because one loves."

*

"This is the hardest of all: to close the open hand out of love, and keep modest as a giver."

*

"Love is blind; friendship closes its eyes."

*

"When marrying, ask yourself this question: Do you believe that you will be able to converse well with this person into your old age? Everything else in marriage is transitory."

*

"A woman may very well form a friendship with a man, but for this to endure, it must be assisted by a little physical antipathy."

*

"There is always some madness in love. But there is also always some reason in madness."

*

"What do I care about the purring of one who cannot love, like the cat?"

*

"Whatever is done for love always occurs beyond good and evil."

*

"Love is not consolation. It is light."

*

"A pair of powerful spectacles has sometimes sufficed to cure a person in love."

*

"Love matches, so called, have illusion for their father and need for their mother."

*

"It is not a lack of love, but a lack of friendship that makes unhappy marriages."

*

"The demand to be loved is the greatest of all arrogant presumptions."

ALSO BY DAVID GRAHAM

Inside the Mind of George Bernard Shaw

The Very Best of Ralph Waldo Emerson

The Very Best of Clint Eastwood

The Very Best of Roger Moore

The Very Best of Kirk Douglas

Printed in Great Britain
by Amazon